_____ Windu sits at

the blue _____.

He has baked a birthday

_____ for Yoda.

The birthday candle is lit.

It has a small _____.

A red bird sits inside a

golden _____.

There is a silver _____

on top of the table.

Boba Fett's Tent

Read the words. Circle the 'e' sound. Choose a word to complete each sentence.

eggs ten nest

tent bed

Boba sits on his *Bed* .

He is inside his *tent* .

There is a bird's *nest* in the tree.

There are *eggs* in the nest.

How many eggs are there?
There are *ten* eggs.

The Queen's Throne Room

The 'ee' sound can be written in many ways, such as ea and ee.

Read the words. Circle the 'ee' sound. Choose a word to complete each sentence.

Queen three feet beak reads green

Queen Amidala sits
on a throne.

Her handmaiden reads
a book.

Her pet bird is
the colour green.

He has yellow feet
and a pink beek.

There are _____ candles
on the small table.

Wicket's Dinner

Read the words. Circle the 'i' sound. Choose a word to complete each sentence.

village   sticks   six

fish   dinner

Wicket lives in a _____
on Endor.

It is early evening, time for
_____.

Wicket uses _____
to make a fire.

How many sticks are there?
_____.

He cooks a big _____.

Qui-Gon's Day

The 'igh' sound can be written in many ways, such as igh, i and i-e.

Read the words. Circle the 'igh' sound. Choose a word to complete each sentence.

white   smiles   hide   behind   ice

Qui-Gon _____.

Jar Jar holds a glass filled with _____.

Padmé plays _____ -and-seek with Anakin.

Anakin hides _____ a bush.

Padmé wears _____ boots.

Anakin's Mum

Anakin lives with his mum, Shmi, near the city of Mos Espa.

Read the words. Circle the 'o' sound. Choose a word to complete each sentence.

Mos sock pot rock hot mop

Anakin and his mum live near

_____ Espa.

Shmi is holding a _____.

There is a big _____ of

soup over the fire.

The fire is very _____.

Anakin is sitting on a

_____.

He is wearing only

one _____.

Yoda's Home

The 'oa' sound can be written in many ways, such as o, o-e and oe.

Read the words. Circle the 'oa' sound. Choose a word to complete each sentence.

oval   stone   robe   note   toes

Yoda wears a long _____ .

Yoda has six _____ .

Yoda uses the Force to make the _____ float.

The stone is the shape of an _____ .

Yoda is writing a _____ to Mace Windu.

Gungans Have Fun!

Read the words. Circle the 'u' sound. Choose a word to complete each sentence.

jumps   umbrella   under

sun   runs

The  is shining brightly.

One Gungan _____.

One Gungan _____.

One Gungan sits _____
a red-and-white _____.

Luke's Uniform

The 'oo' sound can be written in many ways, such as ue, u and u-e.

Read the words. Circle the 'oo' sound. Choose a word to complete each sentence.

Luke

blue

human

dune

uniform

cube

_____ Skywalker wears the
_____ of a Rebel pilot.

He stands on top of
a sand _____.

He holds a small _____
in his hand.

It is the colour _____.

Luke is a _____ being.

Consonants 1

When **r** and another **consonant** are next to each other in a word, you can hear both of their sounds.

Greedo

Here, you can hear both the g and the r sounds.

Read the sounds. Choose the right consonants to complete the words.

cr br tr fr dr pr gr

 ____oom

 ____own

 ____incess

 een

 uit

 unk

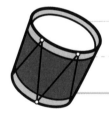 oid

 um

 ee

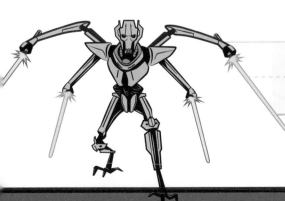 ievous

Consonants 2

When **l** and another **consonant** are next to each other in a word, you can hear both of their sounds.

Plo Koon

Here, you can hear both the **p** and the **l** sounds.

Read the sounds. Choose the right consonants to complete the words.

| pl | gl | sl | cl | bl |

_____ove

_____eep

space_____ug

 aws

 ate

 iers

 obe

 ack

 anket

 ones

Consonants 3

When **s** and another consonant are next to each other in a word, you can hear both of their sounds.

Skywalker

Here, you can hear both the s and the k sounds.

Read the sounds. Choose the right consonants to complete the words.

| sn | sm | sw | sk | sp | st | sc |

_____ ile

_____ ull

_____ ider

ar

y

oke

arf

airs

ail

ing

sh and ch

'Sh' and 'ch' are digraphs. The two letters make one sound.

Shmi

The two letters make
one sound – sh.

Chewbacca

The two letters make
one sound – ch.

Choose 'sh' or 'ch' to complete the words.

ark

air

eep

 erry

 eese

 ell

 irt

 ain

 aak Ti

th, ph and wh

'th', 'ph' and 'wh' are digraphs.
The two letters make one sound.

Darth

th   The two letters make the sound th, as in Darth.

ph   The two letters make the sound f, as in face.

wh   The two letters make the sound w, as in water.

Choose **th, ph** or **wh** to complete the words.

13 _____ irteen

 _____ ip

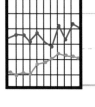 _____ gra

1,000 _____ ousand

 _____ istle

 al _____ abet

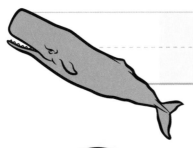 _____ ale

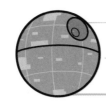 _____ eel

 _____ Dea _____ Star

_____ oto

ai, ay and ey

The 'ai' sound can be written in many ways, such as ai, ay and ey.

Aayla

Here, the a and the y make the long a sound.

Ai and ey also make the long a sound.

Read the words. Circle the 'ai' sound. Choose a word to complete each sentence.

acklay   away   tail   grey   braid

Star Wars takes place a long time ago in a galaxy far, far _____.

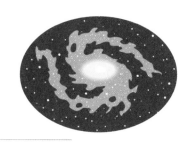

The tauntaun has a long _____.

When white gets dirty,
it looks _____.

Anakin has one _____.

This creature is called
an _____.

ee, ea and ey

The 'ee' sound can be written in many ways, such as ee, ea and ey.

reek

Here, the e and the e make the long e sound.

Ea and ey also make the long e sound.

Read the words. Circle the 'ee' sound. Choose a word to complete each sentence.

money   read   dream

teeth   tree   key

Let's ＿＿＿＿＿＿ a book.

Please brush your ＿＿＿＿＿.

Let's climb up
the _____ .

You need a _____
to unlock a door.

Queen Amidala has a
lot of _____ .

When I sleep, I start
_____
to _____ .

igh and ie

The 'igh' sound can be written in many ways, such as igh and ie.

starfighter

Here, the i, g and h make the long i sound.

ie also makes the long i sound.

Read the words. Circle the 'igh' sound. Choose a word to complete each sentence.

Knight   bright   cries

tie   night   pies

Obi-Wan Kenobi is a Jedi _____.

Please put on your _____.

 The sun is _____ .

The youngling _____ .

 Look at that stack of delicious _____ .

You can see the moon and stars at _____ .

oa and ow

The 'oa' sound can be written in many ways, such as oa and ow.

Owen Lars

Here, the o and the w make the long o sound.

Oa also makes the long o sound.

Choose 'oa' or 'ow' to complete the words.

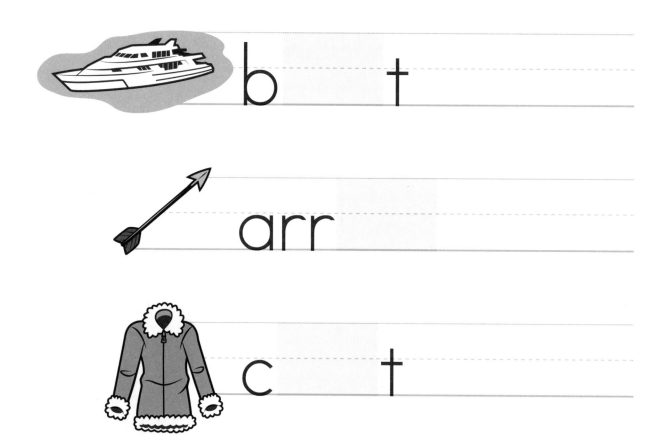

b___t

arr___

c___t

r _____

r _ d

g _ t

gr _____

fl _ t

thr _____

bl _____

ui, ue and ew

The 'oo' sound can be written in many ways, such as ui, ue and ew.

Here, the u and the i make the long u sound.

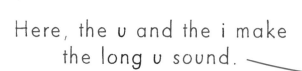

juice

Ue and ew also make the long u sound.

Read the words. Circle the 'oo' sound. Choose a word to complete each sentence.

fruit   blue   glue

new   flew   suit

Jango _____ away.

His helmet is silver

and _____.

The basket is full of _____ .

Luke is wearing a
flight _____ .

Anakin has a _____ droid.

C-3PO needs to _____
the broken jar together.

ar and or

Read the words. Circle the 'ar' sounds
Practise writing the words.

Jar Jar

Jar Jar Jar Jar   Jar Jar

art

far

farm

target

garden

Read the words. Circle the 'or' sounds.
Practise writing the words.

orbit

corn

Sith Lord

fort

torn

Force

horn

er, ir and ur

The 'ir' sound can be written in many ways, such as er, ir and ur. Read the words. Circle the 'ir' sound. Practise writing the words.

Vader

sir _____

fur _____

burn _____

dirt _____

circle _____

Vader _____

girl

fur

herd ....

bird ....

water ....

ruler ....

turn ....

girl ....

surf ....

Soft c and Hard c

The letter **c** makes two different sounds.
The **hard c** makes the **k** sound that you hear in **cat**.
The **soft c** makes the **s** sound that you hear in **city**.

cat

city

Hint: When the letter
c is followed by e,
i or y, it is usually a
soft c

Colour the cards with a **soft c** word in red.
Colour the cards with a **hard c** word in blue.

cage

card

space

cake

cereal

cent

pencil

calendar

Soft g and Hard g

The letter **g** makes two different sounds.

The **hard g** makes the first sound that you hear in **goat**.

The **soft g** makes the **j** sound that you hear in **giraffe**.

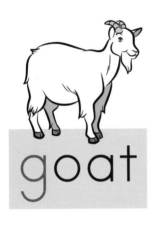

goat

giraffe

Hint: When the letter
g is followed by e,
i or y, it is usually a
soft g

Colour the cards with a **soft g** word in yellow.

Colour the cards with a **hard g** word in green.

orange

gentle

game

general

ago

energy

galaxy

good

Types of Nouns: People

A **noun** stands for a person, place, thing or idea.

Complete each sentence with the correct **noun**.

boy   son   girl   woman   man

The _____ mends the droid.

The _____ has blonde hair.

The _____ and his _____

are in a landspeeder.

The _____ with red hair

waves hello.

Types of Nouns: Places

A **noun** stands for a person, place, thing or idea.

Complete each sentence with the correct **noun**.

forest

mountains

city

lake

desert

The _____ is full
of trees.

The Gungan swims in the

_____ .

There are tall buildings in
the _____ .

There are sand dunes
in the _____ .

There is snow on top of
the _____ .

Types of Nouns: Things

A **noun** stands for a person, place, thing or idea.

Complete each sentence with the correct **noun**.

hammer   trust   droid   goggles

Anakin builds a _____ .

He wears _____ to protect his eyes.

He holds a _____ .

The robot looks at Anakin with _____ in his eyes.

Proper Nouns

A **proper noun** is a word or group of words that names a specific person, place, thing or idea.

A **proper noun** starts with a capital letter.

Underline the **proper nouns** in each sentence.

Han flies the *Millennium Falcon.*

Chewbacca is tall and hairy.

The Death Star is big.

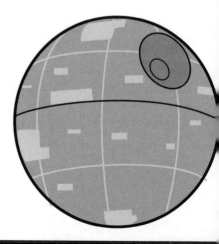

Luke lives on Tatooine.

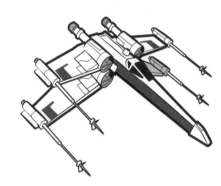 The X-wing is fast.

Wicket lives on Endor.

Go, Wookiee, Go!

A **verb** represents the action in a sentence. It tells us what someone or something does.

Circle the **verb** in each sentence.

The Wookiee eats.

The Wookiee sleeps.

The Wookiee waves.

The Wookiee climbs.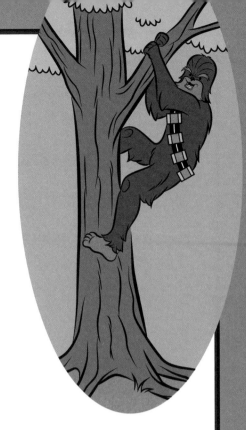

 The Wookiee runs.

The Wookiee builds a droid.

Describe the Creatures!

Read the **adjectives** in the word boxes.

Write the best **adjective** to describe each picture.

blue orange

brown curly

strong white

The Twi'lek has _____ skin and horns.

The _____ Gungan lives on Naboo.

The bantha has
_____ horns.

The _____
wampa lives on Hoth.

The _____
Wookiee is fierce.

The _____ tauntaun
carries heavy loads.

The Youngling's Adventure!

A complete **sentence** has a **subject** and a **verb**. The **subject** of a **sentence** is either a **noun** or a **pronoun**. A **noun** stands for a person, place, thing or idea. A **verb** represents the action in a **sentence**. **Sentences** start with a **capital letter** and end with a **full stop**.

Read this **sentence**:

The orange youngling runs away.

Circle the **noun**. Underline the **verb**.

Draw a triangle around the **capital letter**.

Draw a square around the **full stop** that ends the sentence.

Now copy the sentence below.

Circle the **noun** in this sentence:

The youngling walks.

Underline the **verb** in this sentence:

The youngling sits.

Circle the **noun** and underline the **verb**:

The youngling yawns loudly.

Draw a triangle around the **capital letter** that begins this sentence. Draw a square around the **full stop** that ends this sentence:

A friend sees the youngling.

The Youngling's Day!

These sentences are written incorrectly.

Write each sentence correctly.

the youngling sings.

----

dances the youngling

the runs youngling

The youngling jumps

the youngling sleeps

youngling dives. The

Yoda Questions

Some sentences ask a **question.** A **question** begins with a **capital letter** and ends with a **question mark**. Some questions start with **words**, such as:

who   what   when   where   why   how

Read each question. Underline the question mark and circle the capital letter.

What is Yoda wearing?

Who is Yoda talking to?

Where is Yoda?

How does Yoda look?

When will Yoda go to sleep?

Why is Yoda green?

These sentences are written incorrectly.

Write each sentence correctly.

when will Yoda sit down

<hr>

what colour is Yoda?

<hr>

how old is Yoda

<hr>

who is talking to Yoda

<hr>

This is Yoda

Read about Yoda.

Then answer the questions on the next page.

This is Yoda. Yoda is a Jedi Master.

Yoda is green. He is very old.

Yoda lives in a hut. He uses the Force.

What is Yoda?

Yoda is a _____ .

What colour is Yoda?

Yoda is _____ .

Where does Yoda live?

Yoda lives in a _____ .

What does Yoda use?

Yoda uses the _____ .

Jawas

Read about Jawas.

Then answer the questions on the next page.

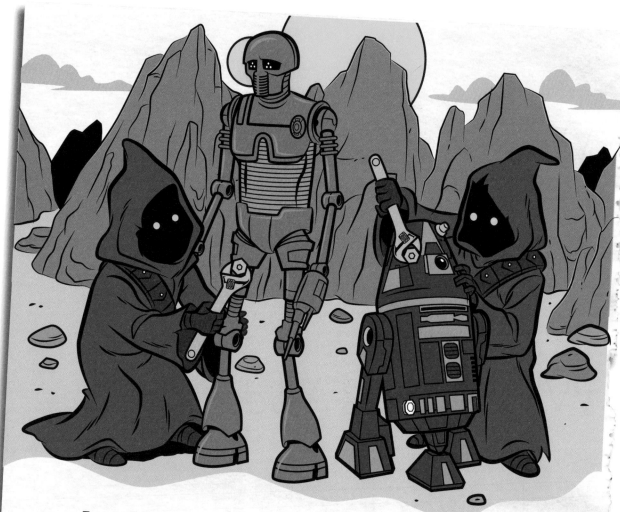

Jawas live in the desert.

They wear brown robes with hoods.

They buy and sell old droids.

These Jawas are fixing some old droids.

The small droid is red and the big droid is blue.

Where do Jawas live?

Jawas live in the ＿＿＿＿＿＿＿＿＿＿.

What do Jawas buy and sell?

Jawas buy and sell ＿＿＿＿＿＿＿.

What colour is the big droid?

The big droid is ＿＿＿＿＿＿.

What colour is the small droid?

The small droid is ＿＿＿＿＿.

Luke Skywalker

Read about Luke.

Then answer the questions on the next page.

Luke Skywalker lives on a desert planet called Tatooine.

He lives on a farm with his aunt and uncle.

He knows that his father was a Jedi Knight.

He does not know that his father's name is Darth Vader.

What is Luke's last name?

Luke's last name is

_____

_____

_____ .

Where does Luke live?

Luke lives on the planet

_____

_____

_____ .

Who is Luke's father?

Luke's father is

_____ _____

_____ _____

_____ _____ .

Princess Leia

Read about Leia.

Then answer the questions on the next page.

Princess Leia sends a message to Obi-Wan Kenobi.

"Help me, Obi-Wan Kenobi!" she says. "You're my only hope."

She puts the message inside R2-D2.

She tells R2-D2 to find Obi-Wan Kenobi and deliver the message.

R2-D2 escapes. He travels to Tatooine to look for Obi-Wan Kenobi.

Put an X in the box with the correct answer.

Who does Princess Leia send a message to?

☐ Obi-Wan Kenobi ☐ R2-D2 ☐ Darth Vader

Where does R2-D2 travel to find Obi-Wan Kenobi?

☐ Tatooine ☐ R2-D2 ☐ Message

What is the name of her droid?

☐ Obi-Wan Kenobi ☐ R2-D2 ☐ Tatooine

R2-D2 and C-3PO

Read about R2-D2 and C-3PO.

Then finish the sentences on the next page.

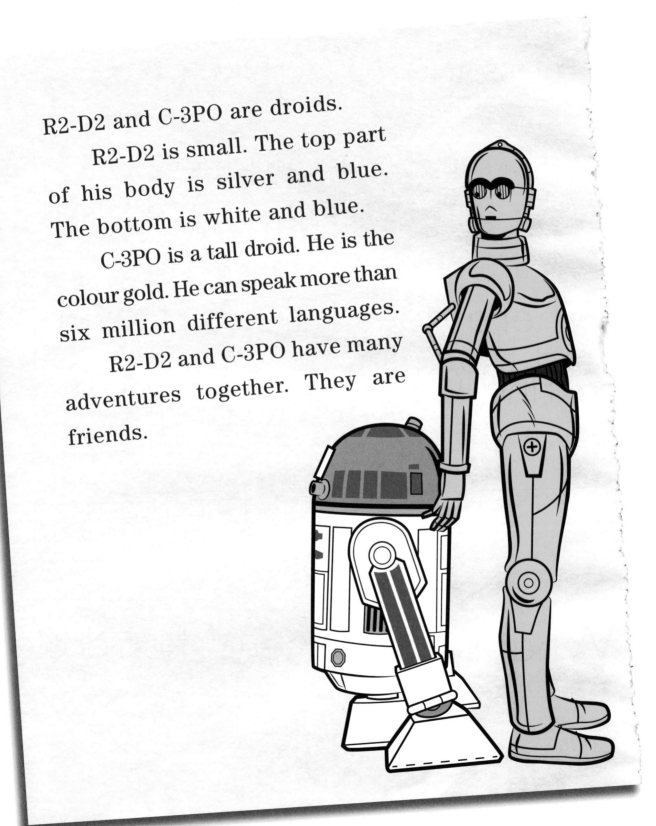

R2-D2 and C-3PO are droids.
R2-D2 is small. The top part of his body is silver and blue. The bottom is white and blue.
C-3PO is a tall droid. He is the colour gold. He can speak more than six million different languages.
R2-D2 and C-3PO have many adventures together. They are friends.

R2-D2 is a type of _____.

C-3PO is not a small droid.
He is _____.

R2-D2 is _____
and blue and white.

C-3PO is the colour _____.

R2-D2 and C-3PO are very
good _____.

Han Solo

Read about Han Solo.

Then write **true** or **false** for the statements on the next page.

Han Solo is a pilot. His starship is called the *Millennium Falcon*. It is very fast. It zooms through the galaxy.

Han Solo flies the *Millennium Falcon* through an asteroid belt. He has to be careful! He can't let an asteroid hit his starship!

Han Solo is a pilot.

The name of Han Solo's starship is the *Millennium Falcon.*

Han Solo does not want an asteroid to hit his starship.

The *Millennium Falcon* is a slow starship.

Chewbacca's World

Read about Chewbacca's world.

Then finish the sentences on the next page.

Chewbacca is a Wookiee. He is very tall and has brown fur. His best friend is Han Solo.

Wookiees come from a jungle planet. It is called Kashyyyk. All Wookiees are very strong.

Wookiees are loyal and gentle friends. When Wookiees get mad, they can be very fierce. You should never make a Wookiee mad at you!

Chewbacca is a very tall

_____ .

Chewbacca has _____ fur.

Chewbacca's best friend

is _____ .

Wookiees are good friends
because they are loyal and

_____ .

When Wookiees are mad,
they can be _____ .

The Jedi Knights

Read about the Jedi Knights.

Then answer the questions on the next page.

Jedi Knights use the Force to protect the galaxy. They have many talents. They are strong and wise. They are very brave.

Jedi Knights live by the Jedi Code, which says that they can only use the Force for good things. They come from all over the galaxy. Obi-Wan Kenobi, Aayla Secura and Mace Windu are all Jedi Knights.

What do Jedi Knights use to protect the galaxy?

They use the _____.

What do Jedi Knights live by?

They live by the _____

_____.

What are the names of the three Jedi Knights in the picture?

The Jedi Knights are:

_____

_____

_____.

Darth Vader and the Force

Read about Darth Vader.

Then finish the sentences on the next page.

Darth Vader was once a Jedi Knight, but he turned to the dark side of the Force. He is very strong. He can use the Force to destroy things. This is not a good use of the Force.

Darth Vader uses a red lightsaber. He wears a black robe and a black helmet. He is very tall. When he walks through his starship, the stormtroopers are all afraid of him. Why are they afraid? They are afraid because Darth Vader can destroy them.

Darth Vader is on the

_____

_____ side of the Force.

The colour of Darth Vader's

lightsaber is _____.

Darth Vader's helmet is

_____

_____ .

The soldiers fear Darth

Vader because he can

_____

_____ .

Lightsabers

Read about lightsabers.

Then answer the questions on the next page.

Lightsabers are blades of pure energy. They can cut through anything – except other lightsabers.

Jedi Knights make their own lightsabers. They use special crystals to give them energy. The colour of the crystal is what gives the lightsaber its colour.

Yoda carries a green lightsaber. Obi-Wan Kenobi's lightsaber is blue. Darth Vader has a red lightsaber.

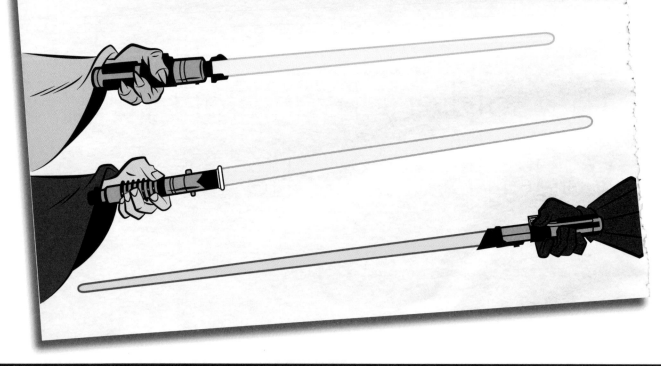

What is a lightsaber made of?

What gives a lightsaber its colour?

What colour is Yoda's lightsaber?

Who carries a red lightsaber?

Who has a blue lightsaber?

Boba Fett

Read about Boba Fett.

Then finish the sentences on the next page.

Boba Fett is a bounty hunter. He wears green armour and carries a blaster. His armour is very special. It lets him do many things that other people cannot do. He can fly with his jetpack. He can also shoot flames.

Boba Fett is very clever. He doesn't talk a lot, though. His father was Jango Fett. Jango was also a bounty hunter.

Boba loved his father and wanted to grow up to be just like him. Now Boba works for Jabba the Hutt. Jabba wants Boba to find Han Solo. If Boba captures Han, Jabba will give him a reward.

Boba Fett is a

_____ hunter.

The colour of Boba's
armour is _____ .

Boba Fett can _____
with his jetpack.

Jango Fett was Boba's

_____ .

Boba is looking for

_____ .

Lando and Lobot

Read the sentences.

Write the correct **feeling** to complete each sentence.

Lando eats a delicious apple.

Lando is _____.

hungry   angry

Lobot lost one of his boots.

Lobot is _____.

upset   excited

Lando sees Darth Vader.

Lando is _____.

scared   glad

Lobot has worked all day and wants to go to bed.

Lobot is _____ .

sleepy   shy

Lando can't wait to see his friend Han Solo.

Lando is _____ .

sad   excited

Lando helps Han Solo escape from Darth Vader.

Lando is _____ .

tired   proud

Answers

page 5

__Anakin__ Skywalker is in the market.

He lives on a __planet__ called Tatooine.

There is a lot of __sand__ in the desert.

The brown __basket__ is full of red __apples__.

It is sunny. Anakin should wear a __hat__.

page 7

__Mace__ Windu sits at the blue __table__.

He has baked a birthday __cake__ for Yoda.

The birthday candle is lit. It has a small __flame__.

A red bird sits inside a golden __cage__.

There is a silver __chain__ on top of the table.

page 9

Boba sits on his __bed__.

He is inside his __tent__.

There is a bird's __nest__ in the tree.

There are __eggs__ in the nest.

How many eggs are there? There are __ten__ eggs.

page 11

__Queen__ Amidala sits on a throne.

Her handmaiden __reads__ a book.

Her pet bird is the colour __green__.

He has yellow __feet__ and a pink __beak__.

There are __three__ candles on the small table.

page 13

Wicket lives in a __village__ on Endor.

It is early evening, time for __dinner__.

Wicket uses __sticks__ to make a fire.

How many sticks are there? __six__.

He cooks a big __fish__.

page 15

Qui-Gon __smiles__.

Jar Jar holds a glass filled with __ice__.

Padmé plays __hide__-and-seek with Anakin.

Anakin hides __behind__ a bush.

Padmé wears __white__ boots.

page 17

Anakin and his mum live near __Mos__ Espa.

Shmi is holding a __mop__.

There is a big __pot__ of soup over the fire.

The fire is very __hot__.

Anakin is sitting on a __rock__.

He is wearing only one __sock__.

page 19

Yoda wears a long __robe__.

Yoda has six __toes__.

Yoda uses the Force to make the __stone__ float.

The stone is the shape of an __oval__.

Yoda is writing a __note__ to Mace Windu.

page 21

The __sun__ is shining brightly.

One Gungan __runs__.

One Gungan __jumps__.

One Gungan sits __under__ a red-and-white __umbrella__.

page 23

__Luke__ Skywalker wears the __uniform__ of a Rebel pilot.

He stands on top of a sand __dune__.

He holds a small __cube__ in his hand.

It is the colour __blue__.

Luke is a __human__ being.

pages 24–25

Consonants 1

When r and another **consonant** are next to each other in a word, you can hear both of their sounds.

Greedo

Here, you can hear both the **g** and the **r** sounds.

Read the sounds. Choose the right consonants to complete the words.

cr br tr fr dr pr gr

__broom__

__crown__

__princess__

__green__

__fruit__

__trunk__

__droid__

__drum__

__tree__

__grievous__

pages 26–27

Consonants 2

When l and another **consonant** are next to each other in a word, you can hear both of their sounds.

Plo Koon

Here, you can hear both the **p** and the **l** sounds.

Read the sounds. Choose the right consonants to complete the words.

pl gl sl cl bl

__glove__

__sleep__

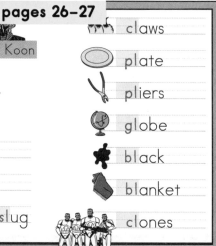__space__ __slug__

__claws__

__plate__

__pliers__

__globe__

__black__

__blanket__

__clones__

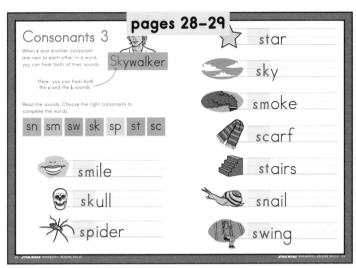

Consonants 3

When s and another consonant are next to each other in a word, you can hear both of their sounds.

Skywalker

Here, you can hear both the s and the k sounds.

Read the sounds. Choose the right consonants to complete the words.

| sn | sm | sw | sk | sp | st | sc |

smile

skull

spider

star

sky

smoke

scarf

stairs

snail

swing

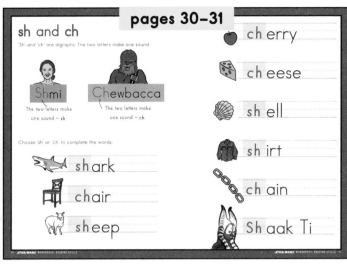

sh and ch

'Sh' and 'ch' are digraphs. The two letters make one sound.

Shmi
The two letters make one sound – sh.

Chewbacca
The two letters make one sound – ch.

Choose 'sh' or 'ch' to complete the words.

shark

chair

sheep

ch erry

ch eese

sh ell

sh irt

ch ain

Sh aak Ti

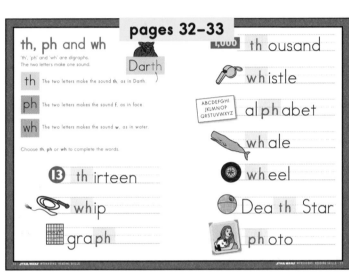

th, ph and wh

'th', 'ph' and 'wh' are digraphs. The two letters make one sound.

Darth

th The two letters make the sound th, as in Darth.

ph The two letters makes the sound f, as in face.

wh The two letters makes the sound w, as in water.

Choose th, ph or wh to complete the words.

⑬ th irteen

whip

graph

th ousand

whistle

al ph abet

wh ale

wheel

Dea th Star

ph oto

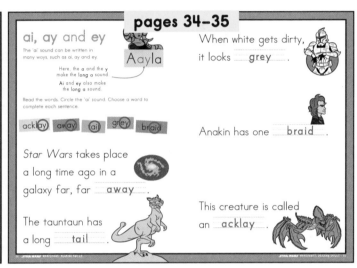

ai, ay and ey

The 'ai' sound can be written in many ways, such as ai, ay and ey.

Aayla

Here, the a and the y make the long a sound.
Ai and ey also make the long a sound.

Read the words. Circle the 'ai' sound. Choose a word to complete each sentence.

ackl(ay)   away   (ai)   grey   braid

Star Wars takes place a long time ago in a galaxy far, far **away** .

The tauntaun has a long **tail** .

When white gets dirty, it looks **grey** .

Anakin has one **braid** .

This creature is called an **acklay** .

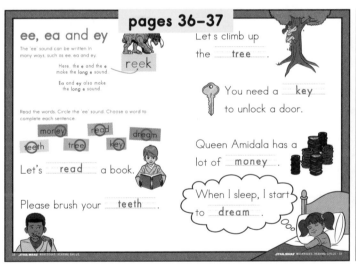

ee, ea and ey

The 'ee' sound can be written in many ways, such as ee, ea and ey.

reek

Here, the e and the e make the long e sound.
Ea and ey also make the long e sound.

Read the words. Circle the 'ee' sound. Choose a word to complete each sentence.

money   re(ad)   dream
t(ee)th   (tree)   k(ey)

Let's **read** a book.

Please brush your **teeth** .

Let's climb up the **tree** .

You need a **key** to unlock a door.

Queen Amidala has a lot of **money** .

When I sleep, I start to **dream** .

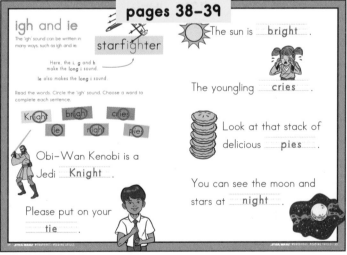

igh and ie

The 'igh' sound can be written in many ways, such as igh and ie.

starfighter

Here, the i, g and h make the long i sound.
Ie also makes the long i sound.

Read the words. Circle the 'igh' sound. Choose a word to complete each sentence.

Kn(igh)t   br(igh)t   cries
(ie)   n(igh)t   pies

Obi-Wan Kenobi is a Jedi **Knight** .

Please put on your **tie** .

The sun is **bright** .

The youngling **cries** .

Look at that stack of delicious **pies** .

You can see the moon and stars at **night** .

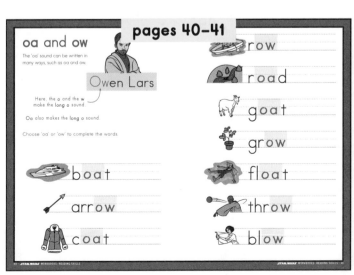

oa and ow

The 'oo' sound can be written in many ways, such as oa and ow.

Owen Lars

Here, the o and the w make the long o sound.

Oa also makes the long o sound.

Choose 'oa' or 'ow' to complete the words.

b oat

arr ow

c oat

r ow

r oad

g oat

gr ow

fl oat

thr ow

bl ow

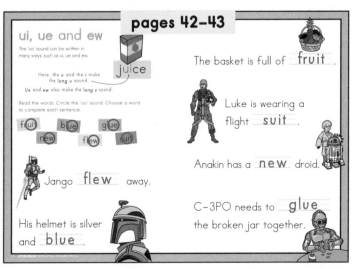

ui, ue and ew

The 'oo' sound can be written in many ways, such as ui, ue and ew.

juice

Here, the u and the i make the long u sound.
Ue and ew also make the long u sound.

Read the words. Circle the 'oo' sound. Choose a word to complete each sentence.

fr(ui)t   bl(ue)   gl(ue)
n(ew)   fl(ew)   s(ui)t

Jango **flew** away.

His helmet is silver and **blue** .

The basket is full of **fruit** .

Luke is wearing a flight **suit** .

Anakin has a **new** droid.

C-3PO needs to **glue** the broken jar together.

Answers

pages 44–45

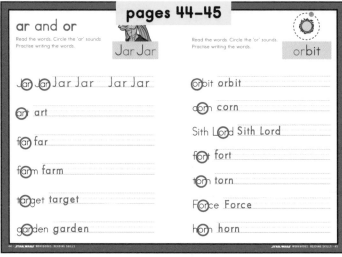

ar and or

Read the words. Circle the 'ar' sounds.
Practise writing the words.

Jar Jar

(Jar) (Jar) Jar Jar   Jar Jar

(ar)t art

(far) far

(far)m farm

(tar)get target

(gar)den garden

Read the words. Circle the 'or' sounds.
Practise writing the words.

orbit

(or)bit orbit

(cor)n corn

Sith L(or)d Sith Lord

(for)t fort

(tor)n torn

F(or)ce Force

(hor)n horn

pages 46–47

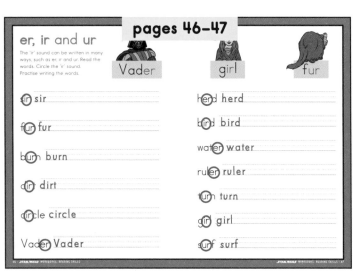

er, ir and ur

The 'ir' sound can be written in many
ways, such as er, ir and ur. Read the
words. Circle the 'ir' sound.
Practise writing the words.

Vader   girl   fur

(ir) sir

f(ur) fur

b(ur)n burn

d(ir)t dirt

c(ir)cle circle

Vad(er) Vader

h(er)d herd

b(ir)d bird

wat(er) water

rul(er) ruler

t(ur)n turn

g(ir)l girl

s(ur)f surf

pages 48–49

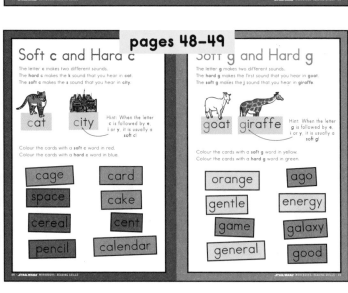

Soft c and Hard c

The letter c makes two different sounds.
The **hard c** makes the k sound that you hear in **cat**.
The **soft c** makes the s sound that you hear in **city**.

cat   city

Hint: When the letter
c is followed by e,
i or y, it is usually a
soft c!

Colour the cards with a **soft c** word in red.
Colour the cards with a **hard c** word in blue.

cage   card
space   cake
cereal   cent
pencil   calendar

Soft g and Hard g

The letter g makes two different sounds.
The **hard g** makes the first sound that you hear in **goat**.
The **soft g** makes the j sound that you hear in **giraffe**.

goat   giraffe

Hint: When the letter
g is followed by e,
i or y, it is usually a
soft g!

Colour the cards with a **soft g** word in yellow.
Colour the cards with a **hard g** word in green.

orange   ago
gentle   energy
game   galaxy
general   good

pages 50–51

Types of Nouns: People

A **noun** stands for a person, place, thing or idea.
Complete each sentence with the correct **noun**.

boy son girl woman man

The ___girl___ mends the droid.

The ___woman___ has blonde hair.

The ___man___ and his ___son___
are in a landspeeder.

The ___boy___ with red hair
waves hello.

page 53

The ___forest___ is full
of trees.

The Gungan swims in the
___lake___.

There are tall buildings in
the ___city___.

There are sand dunes
in the ___desert___.

There is snow on top of
the ___mountains___.

page 55

Anakin builds a ___droid___.

He wears ___goggles___ to
protect his eyes.

He holds a ___hammer___.

The robot looks at Anakin
with ___trust___ in his eyes.

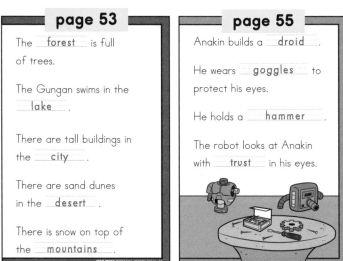

pages 56–57

Proper Nouns

A **proper noun** is a word or group of words that names a
specific person, place, thing or idea.
A **proper noun** starts with a capital letter.
Underline the **proper nouns** in each sentence.

Han flies the _Millennium Falcon_.

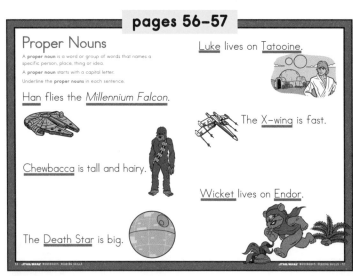

Chewbacca is tall and hairy.

Luke lives on Tatooine.

The X-wing is fast.

Wicket lives on Endor.

The Death Star is big.

pages 58–59

Go, Wookiee, Go!

A **verb** represents the action in a sentence. It tells us what
someone or something does.
Circle the **verb** in each sentence.

The Wookiee (eats).

The Wookiee (sleeps).

The Wookiee (waves).

The Wookiee (climbs).

The Wookiee (runs).

The Wookiee (builds) a droid.

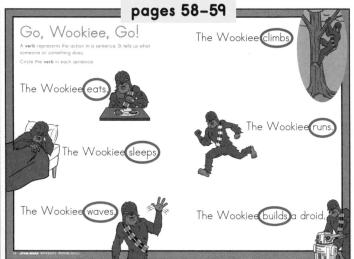

pages 60–61

Describe the Creatures:

Read the adjectives in the word boxes.
Write the best adjective to describe each picture.

Word box: blue, orange, brown, curly, strong, white

The bantha has **curly** horns.

The **white** wampa lives on Hoth.

The Twi'lek has **blue** skin and horns.

The **brown** Wookiee is fierce.

The **orange** Gungan lives on Naboo.

The **strong** tauntaun carries heavy loads.

pages 62–63

The Youngling's Adventure!

A complete sentence has a subject and a verb. The subject of a sentence is either a noun or a pronoun. A noun stands for a person, place, thing or idea. A verb represents the action in a sentence. Sentences start with a capital letter and end with a full stop.

Read this sentence:

The orange (youngling) runs away.

Circle the noun. Underline the verb.
Draw a triangle around the capital letter.
Draw a square around the full stop that ends the sentence.
Now copy the sentence below.

Circle the noun in this sentence:
The (youngling) walks.

Underline the verb in this sentence:
The youngling sits.

Circle the noun and underline the verb:
The (youngling) yawns loudly.

Draw a triangle around the capital letter that begins this sentence. Draw a square around the full stop that ends this sentence:
A friend sees the youngling.

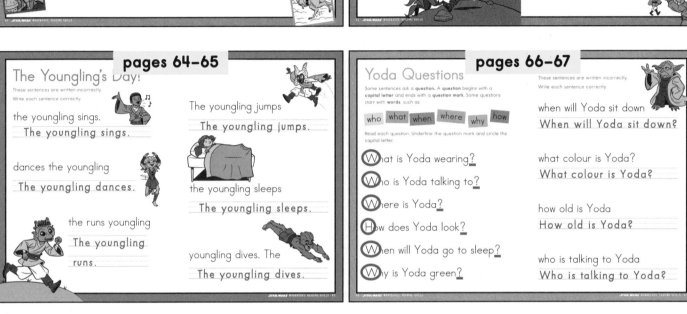

pages 64–65

The Youngling's Day!

These sentences are written incorrectly.
Write each sentence correctly.

the youngling sings.
The youngling sings.

dances the youngling
The youngling dances.

the runs youngling
The youngling runs.

The youngling jumps
The youngling jumps.

the youngling sleeps
The youngling sleeps.

youngling dives. The
The youngling dives.

pages 66–67

Yoda Questions

Some sentences ask a question. A question begins with a capital letter and ends with a question mark. Some questions start with words, such as:

who what when where why how

Read each question. Underline the question mark and circle the capital letter.

(W)hat is Yoda wearing?
(W)ho is Yoda talking to?
(W)here is Yoda?
(H)ow does Yoda look?
(W)hen will Yoda go to sleep?
(W)hy is Yoda green?

These sentences are written incorrectly.
Write each sentence correctly.

when will Yoda sit down
When will Yoda sit down?

what colour is Yoda?
What colour is Yoda?

how old is Yoda
How old is Yoda?

who is talking to Yoda
Who is talking to Yoda?

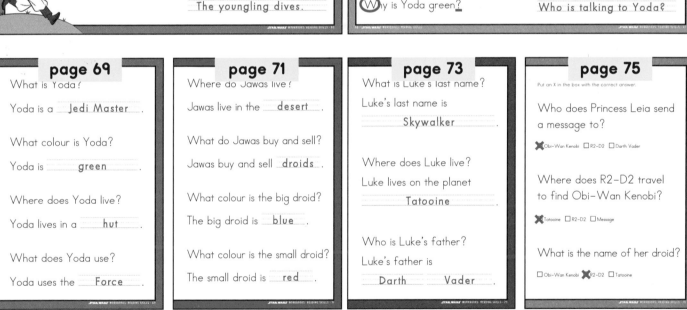

page 69

What is Yoda?
Yoda is a **Jedi Master**.

What colour is Yoda?
Yoda is **green**.

Where does Yoda live?
Yoda lives in a **hut**.

What does Yoda use?
Yoda uses the **Force**.

page 71

Where do Jawas live?
Jawas live in the **desert**.

What do Jawas buy and sell?
Jawas buy and sell **droids**.

What colour is the big droid?
The big droid is **blue**.

What colour is the small droid?
The small droid is **red**.

page 73

What is Luke's last name?
Luke's last name is **Skywalker**.

Where does Luke live?
Luke lives on the planet **Tatooine**.

Who is Luke's father?
Luke's father is **Darth Vader**.

page 75

Put an X in the box with the correct answer.

Who does Princess Leia send a message to?
☒ Obi-Wan Kenobi ☐ R2-D2 ☐ Darth Vader

Where does R2-D2 travel to find Obi-Wan Kenobi?
☒ Tatooine ☐ R2-D2 ☐ Message

What is the name of her droid?
☐ Obi-Wan Kenobi ☒ R2-D2 ☐ Tatooine

page 77

R2-D2 is a type of **droid**.

C-3PO is not a small droid. He is **tall**.

R2-D2 is **silver** and blue and white.

C-3PO is the colour **gold**.

R2-D2 and C-3PO are very good **friends**.

page 79

Han Solo is a pilot. **true**

The name of Han Solo's starship is the *Millennium Falcon*. **true**

Han Solo does not want an asteroid to hit his starship. **true**

The *Millennium Falcon* is a slow starship. **false**

page 81

Chewbacca is a very tall **Wookiee**.

Chewbacca has **brown** fur.

Chewbacca's best friend is **Han Solo**.

Wookiees are good friends because they are loyal and **gentle**.

When Wookiees are mad, they can be **fierce**.

page 83

What do Jedi Knights use to protect the galaxy?
They use the **Force**.

What do Jedi Knights live by?
They live by the **Jedi Code**.

What are the names of the three Jedi Knights in the picture?
The Jedi Knights are:
Obi-Wan Kenobi, Aayla Secura and Mace Windu.

Answers

Darth Vader is on the
___dark___ side of the Force.

The colour of Darth Vader's
lightsaber is ___red___ .

Darth Vader's helmet is
___black___ .

The soldiers fear Darth
Vader because he can
___destroy them___

What is a lightsaber made
of? ___pure energy___

What gives a lightsaber
its colour?
___special crystals___

What colour is Yoda's
lightsaber? ___green___

Who carries a red lightsaber?
___Darth Vader___

Who has a blue lightsaber?
___Obi-Wan Kenobi___

Boba Fett is a
___bounty___ hunter.

The colour of Boba's
armour is ___green___ .

Boba Fett can ___fly___
with his jetpack.

Jango Fett was Boba's
___father___ .

Boba is looking for
___Han Solo___ .

Lando and Lobot

Read the sentences.

Write the correct **feeling** to complete each sentence.

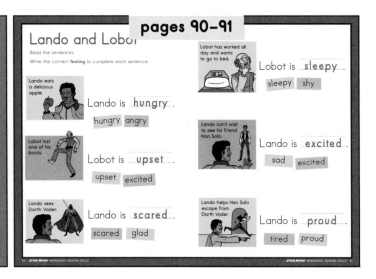

Lando eats a delicious apple.
Lando is ___hungry___ .
hungry   angry

Lobot lost one of his boots.
Lobot is ___upset___ .
upset   excited

Lando sees Darth Vader.
Lando is ___scared___ .
scared   glad

Lobot has worked all day and wants to go to bed.
Lobot is ___sleepy___ .
sleepy   shy

Lando can't wait to see his friend Han Solo.
Lando is ___excited___ .
sad   excited

Lando helps Han Solo escape from Darth Vader.
Lando is ___proud___ .
tired   proud